FENG SHUI

FENG SHUI

Harry Rolnick

You ask why I live in the
green mountains.

I laugh and don't reply,
for my heart is at peace.

Like the peach blossoms
in the stream, I calmly
flow away.

To another sky,
another earth.

FormAsia

Feng Shui: The Chinese System of Elements

Published by:
FormAsia Books Limited
706, Yu Yuet Lai Building
45, Wyndham Street
Central, Hong Kong
www.formasiabooks.com

Published 2004
ISBN 962-7283-84-3
Text and photographs © FormAsia Books Limited

Written by Harry Rolnick
Art Direction by Hans Lindberg
Edited by Peter Sherwood
Proofread by Jamie Cox

Digital Artwork by Kitty Chan
FormAsia Marketing by Eliza Chan
Photography by FormAsia Books
Camera Assistant: Sathish Gobinath
Page 102-103: National Geographic Magazine

Printed in Hong Kong
Printed by Sing Cheong Printing Company Limited
Film separations by Sky Art Graphic Co., Limited

CONTENTS

1

PRELUDE

Mozart and the Magic Ch'i

For as long as people have wondered about thunder, lightning, life and after-life, humankind in the West has tried to pack the endless mysteries of the universe into one sacred shopping bag. Its divine panacea was labelled God, Karma, Fate, or The-Way-The-Cookie-Crumbles. Traditional Chinese beliefs have an alternative way of solving natural

Water is the first of the Five Elements. Fire, wood, earth and metal complete the line-up. Canals in the early ages were built to salvage the country from the Great Flood.

Mozart (insert) wrote compositions based on feng shui elements of chance.

mysteries. Since 8,000 BCE (Before the Common Era), Chinese philosophers have decreed that certain cosmic riddles are insoluble. Thus, instead of trying to solve the mysteries of the universe, we should live in harmony with these enigmas. Rather than tampering with nature, we should, in the words of Voltaire, "plant our garden and let our flowers grow".

That garden, though, is the garden of our mind, indivisible from the gardens of nature. Feng shui, then, is not a sacred phrase; it simply means 'wind and water'.

By embracing the cosmos, we should flow with the current, of wind, water and every other object in our life. Like a Mozart opera or a Ferrari engine, we needn't understand the mechanics to be transported by its effect. Like the Tao of the famed Tao Te-ching, if we understand too much, then it isn't really feng shui at all.

Feng shui is the term used to define the geomantic system by which the orientation of sites, of houses, cities, graves, etc., is determined and the agreeable and disagreeable luck of families and communities is pre-ordained.

The dousing-rod and the astrological compass are employed for this purpose.

This flow that regulates our lives is an invisible

energy known as ch'i (or 'qi' for Scrabble-players). To partake in this energy, we can arrange our inner nature and our outer environment to allow it to flow like water or drift like the wind, and provide us with benefits rather than harm. We cannot control the wind, but we can however arrange our lives so this 'energy' benefits us.

Traditionally, if ch'i has an unobstructed passage, it may whiz right by us without providing stimulus. If on the other hand the passage has too many negative obstacles to overcome, the energy may be delayed and be depleted of its power to energize. With the right configuration of our inner and outer environments, ch'i allows us to live our lives to the fullest.

Although feng shui offers us alternative solutions to optimize this environment, no single right or wrong path achieves these effects. The Judeo-Christian-Islamic tradition preaches good and evil, right and wrong. Feng

shui to the contrary does not accept the concept of such extremes: Dark turns into light, feminine into masculine, gentle turns aggressive. The 'positive' sheng ch'i and 'negative' shar ch'i actually complement each other; just as the symbol of yin-yang turns into itself like a helix. One generates vitality, the other calm and peace, and too much of either results in hyperactivity or lassitude, so a balance must be reached.

While the West offers problems and solutions, feng shui offers situations, and these can be altered for the better. By means of talismans and charms the unpropitious character of any particular topography may be satisfactorily counteracted.

The situation is universal, since feng shui is in everything and connects with everything. It changes and can be changed. Some claim that our environment is influenced by our date of birth, balancing our stars and ourselves. Others call simply for the right sounds, colours, balances of organic (fish, flowers, moss, vegetation, etc.,) with non-organic (furniture, sculpture, pictures, etc.,).

One configures these objects to blend into one's natural space.

Feng shui paradoxically believes in an attitude of fate, where the fate of our will and that of the heavens work in tandem.

Tien chai means the fate of heaven: the sphere

of astrology. For true believers, this is sacrosanct and cannot be altered.

Ti chai represents our environment, creating the 'right' space. This implies trying to mould our own universe to suit us.

The following chapters offer directions – if not rules.

Ren chai is the luck of Humankind: the way we are. It is free-will, the will to shape ourselves.

Perhaps the best way to view our life in feng shui terms is less like a game of chess, which is reliant on intelligence, or a game of roulette which is pure luck.

Life tends to emulate the game of backgammon: The roll of dice is luck, but we have the ability to optimize what luck has dealt us. This then is neither fate nor free will, but the ability to shape our fate by exercising our will.

Feng shui also has several 'sects', but they are not in

Feng shui's origins date back to predictions based on the tossing of animal bones. Dice are its modern innovation, but extend the same custom of interpreting signs in a universe of endless answers.

competition with each other. Each sect simply 'sees another mountain', as a Chinese sage put it. The earliest sect, the 'Form and Landscape sect', interprets the physical aspects of our home and surroundings by means of the symbols of animals and elements. If fortunate, we will be surrounded by space, trees, mountains and rivers. Conversely, if less fortunate in an urban environment, these elements are replicated by congestion, roads, buildings and things artificial like ponds, parks and waterfalls to guide or deflect the ch'i.

The dragon symbolises all that is powerful in China – from the Emperor to the booming whoosh of hurricane winds. It is the emblem of vigilance and roof-ridges are protected from evil by its benevolence.

The 'Compass School sect', is more technical, since a compass, protractor and meticulous graphs, as well as auspicious days determine a configuration. Feng shui practitioners of this discipline are mathematically inclined and have the minds of structural engineers. Though it must be said a great deal of 'magic' goes along with this science.

Essentially, our personal, environmental and cosmic future is not reliant on a single truth or sacred knowledge. We simply work with the energy dealt us and that which we receive, to establish a life-enhancing truth for ourselves.

Dragons are associated with flowing water. As in any Western arrangement, the fusion of man-made and heaven-created motifs relaxes both mind and body.

Some say gargoyles that embellish Gothic architecture originated from Chinese temple statuary. The charming pandemonium of the pantheon of a village temple is captured in glazed porcelain from Shekwan Province.

16

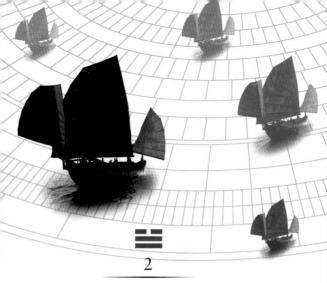

2

HISTORY

From Eternity to Here

Most religious beliefs derive from revelations through an enlightened individual.

Feng shui, though, came from no single divine revelation. Instead, it is the product of thousands of years of maritime science, philosophy, and aesthetics, extending even to landscape gardening.

Among the first to navigate the oceans, the Chinese deduced that the moon – exercising direct influence on the currents – could also influence our lives. This energy extended to the entire universe, all peoples including those anestors who had passed on.

Taiwanese artist Ju Ming's powerful Tai Chi sculpture embodies traits of the 'great energy' with the added merit of standing in the propitious element of water.

This appreciation – and later Confucian worship – of family is an essential component of Chinese life. By utilizing these universal energies, our forefathers could be assured a propitious burial, so no matter where they resided in the afterlife, they would be cared for on earth. This comfort had to encompass the salubrious cooling powers of wind and the eternal flowing energies of water. And thus began the burial practices of feng shui and, later, architectural principles for our homes and the urban environment as described in official texts of the Shang Dynasty (1755-1046 BCE).

From the Sixth century to First century BCE, feng shui expanded in theory and practice. The Tao Te-ching, the book of Sixth century maxims, taught that academic scholarship was close to futile – only the Tao (or Way) could bring contentment. Priests were as taboo as teachers, but almost inevitably priests of the Taoist belief, with their New Age knowledge, wrote countless books of spells and almanacs which later formed one school of feng shui.

Feng shui consistently recognised water as China's most positive element, embracing abundance and fortune. Water at the threshold of a homestead similarly implies an endless flow of wealth.

These books also included a unique oracular teaching called the I-Ching, which originated when a mythical king dreamed of magical marks on an animal's back. Each mark had varying layers, which the king divined to imply heaven, earth and thunder. While the Book of Changes wasn't published until 1122 BCE, feng shui oracles had been using it to predict and counsel their believers for untold years.

In theory, the I-Ching was magic, but it included

In a posture of reverence, Gautama the Buddha is seen preaching to his disciples. Feng shui does not limit itself to a single belief, but displays equal reverence for all teachings.

two extremely notable elements important in today's feng shui. First, one's particular markings were achieved by throwing dice on the ground and divining a reading. Thus, one depended on using one's chance for maximum effect. Second, the predictions were never specific. They were couched in terms that could have manifold meanings.

Two other philosophers were peripheral to feng shui. Gautama the Buddha offered the wisdom of moderation in all things, which became part of the balance of energies. Confucius, while more of a political philosopher, believed in the traditional acceptance of earthly situations as well as reverence for our forebears.

By the Tang Dynasty (618-907 CE), scholars were required to study all the existing oracular books, learning the philosophy and rituals by rote. Far from producing scholars, these studies produced pliant administrators who had lost the ability to reason. Even scientific discoveries were made to assist the priestly classes, rather than to benefit society as a whole.

Consequently, the intelligentsia covertly ridiculed feng shui. That secrecy became public when an 18th century satirist, Wu Ching-tzu, published a book akin to Gulliver's Travels, mocking religious traditions

Wu satirically described Feng Shui 'merchants' contemplating the site of a grave. They studiously examine clods of earth. They break off pieces of dirt, they taste them, swirl them around like wine, and make the grand announcement:

Wisdom in China was passed down in written form, in volumes pored over by scholars who believed that scripted characters were almost sacrosanct.

"A burial here will only bankrupt your family". At the next site, a Feng Shui priest is more optimistic. "A burial here will produce a Number One graduate in your family". He accepts from the grief-stricken family his fees for his insight and time and moves on. The book refers to Feng Shui as 'charlatanism', and its priests as 'quarrelsome scroungers'.

While widely practised in the countryside, since 1949 the Chinese Communist Party has officially described priests as bogus, "springing atop houses, becoming young, turning grey beards to black, surviving the hottest days without perspiring, the

coldest without shivering". Unofficially, though, certain practices could never totally be eliminated. For example, when the Bank of China was erected in the Portuguese colony of Macau, its main façade fronted a statue of a Portuguese governor, and the sword he held, on a public square half a mile away. The Chinese dismantled the statue, ostensibly for 'political' reasons since the territory was soon to be returned to Chinese sovereignty anyway. The feng shui reality remains that geomancers had advised that the Bank's recent misfortunes were the result of 'poison arrows' aimed at it by the Portuguese.

As a counter-reaction to the official party line, refugees brought the feng shui philosophy to the world, like the initial secrets of silk production smuggled out of China in a hollowed-out walking stick by a Jesuit priest. As with acupuncture, Westerners soon became intrigued with the restorative powers and rituals of feng shui.

Today, aside from the burial practices in mainland China, the main practitioners reside in Hong Kong and the United States, where feng shui has become a hallmark of New Agers, business tycoons, movie stars, housewives and artists. The geomancy-crystal ball industry has become big business indeed.

The Pagoda –
Sanskrit Stupa –
meaning Relic of the
Preserver. Pagodas
have varying
spiritual destinies:
they can either repel
floodwaters, bestow
fortunes or repulse
the approach of
the barbarian
hoards from the
Mongol north.

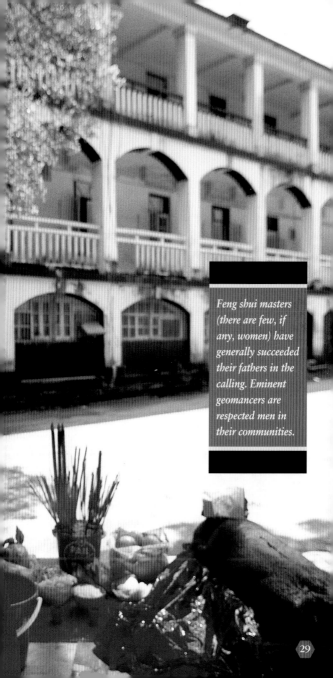

Feng shui masters (there are few, if any, women) have generally succeeded their fathers in the calling. Eminent geomancers are respected men in their communities.

29

Lao-tse believed that walking in the clouds brought one closer to heavenly powers than studying the works of Mandarin scholars, as embodied by Wallace Stevens in his poem.

3

FORM

Landscape, and Your Dragon's Lair

Feng shui doctrine is encapsulated in a saying from the Book of Burial: "Ch'i blows as wind, ascends to the clouds, falls as rain, nourishes the soil and gives birth to everything on earth." Since

"The garden flew round with the angel,
The angel flew round with the clouds,
and the clouds flew round and the
clouds flew round with the clouds."

Wallace Stevens

energy is the universe, the goal of feng shui is not to obstruct or harness it. We build our lives with nature, enriching ourselves with its bounty. Feng shui offers no single set of rules; it just flows. Observe the flowing of the yin/yang symbol. It too has no beginning nor end nor foreground nor background. Like Einstein's circular universe, everything gracefully and endlessly flows back to its source... like wind, like water.

Feng shui has two definitive principles: The Form/Landscape discipline and the Compass discipline.

The Form/Landscape School is environmentally and ecologically savvy. Although mythological animals are engaged to describe your home-site they have become metaphors, pictorial signposts that aided a once illiterate population.

Paradoxically, the Compass School uses actual tools, but the tools are aids for magical formulae that were interpreted by the professional priest or geomancer a very long time ago.

Form/Landscape deals mainly with the correct siting and structure for your home. These should encompass seven natural elements: mountains, water, soil, direction, wind, time and land-shape. But 21st century reality is obliged to make compromises – based on intuition and natural balance.

Therefore mountains can be interpreted as surrounding buildings, which offer security. Water can be the Pacific Ocean, a stream or a goldfish pond. Soil is the flesh of your house's body; your land should be fertile, loamy, rich with the nutrients for planting flowers. Direction and wind are in tandem. Your house should face the south, 'from whence cometh the balmiest winds'.

Timing has two meanings: In the Compass School (Chapter Four) your birth date determines when you should relocate, build, and alter your life, while in Form/Landscape school, logic is required.

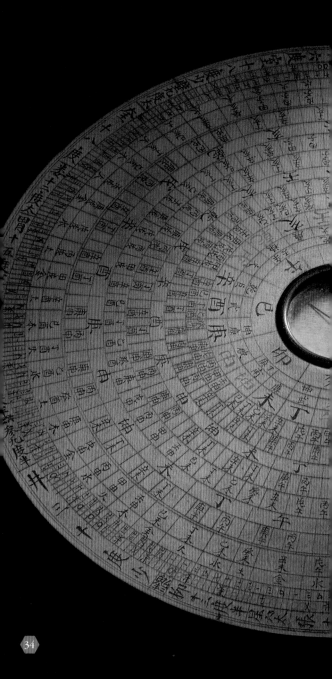

The most important feng shui instrument is the astrological compass. It offers both good and harmful guidelines, malevolent influences and propitious numbers. Incidentally it also provides directions!

You should be aware and conscious of what is most comfortable in your financial, emotional and physical circumstances, rather than using an arbitrary date on which to select your site.

Once you locate your property or an apartment house that nestles comfortably between stream and mountains, or urban structures and artificial ponds, you have your land-shape. When ideally sited, this is known as the 'dragon's lair', since the dragon is the most magnificent creature in Chinese mythology. The ideal site should be located at 'the tail of the dragon', the foot of a mountain range or at the base of protective surrounding urban area.

Remember that in feng shui, this balance is applicable to houses, bodies.

And entire cities. Kowloon, the name for the mountain range separating mainland China from Hong Kong means 'nine dragons', named after Kowloon's eight predominant peaks in the range. The ninth 'dragon' title is reserved exclusively for the Emperor.

The second step is actually building your house, and for this feng shui dubs you with an Auspicious Number. Since that number signifies everything in your life, it becomes important, and several equations can solve the problem. One easy way is to take the final number of your year of birth, although feng shui magicians might offer other equations for this number. Here the 'magic' again comes to play.

Significant corresponding elements and what they connote are listed below:

0, 1: Metal *(precision, finance, clarity of thought)*

2, 3: Water *(knowledge, arts, flexibility)*

4, 5: Wood *(ambition, productivity, advertising)*

6, 7: Fire *(excitement, academia, risk)*

8, 9: Earth *(Space, stability, tranquillity)*

Alternatively, instead of a lucky number, think of your own dominant mood, or the element you intuitively are drawn to, then build accordingly.

Water and Wood people tend to be nature lovers who thrive in forests or near the pounding sea. Metal people are cast to being close to the action, while Fire-folks are motivated by the heat and excitement of imaginative places with shapes and forms. Earth people require very little; fewer mountains, more landscapes and ample open spaces.

'Compass-ites' assert that the Five Elements have constructive and destructive interactive powers. Constructively, Wood enhances Fire, Fire leaves Earth, Earth creates Metal, Metal is liquefied to Water, Water nurtures Wood, and back to the beginning.

Destructively, Water douses Fire, Fire melts Metal, Metal destroys Wood, Wood devours nutriments from the Earth, Earth quenches Water.

Your house shape will hardly be akin to

China's mountains have defended it against 'barbarian invasions' since the beginning of nationhood. In feng shui terms, mountains serve the same purpose of defence against unfavourable elements.

traditional Chinese house rectangles, but certain shapes should be avoided. For instance, an L-formed structure resembles a Chinese meat cleaver (very dangerous!). A U-shaped house ushers in unhappiness, since the energy flows idly around, like stagnant air.

But feng shui does not have rules set in stone, nor cast in concrete nor cemented with bricks. In case the ideal symmetry of your home cannot be attained, you can remedy the situation with landscaping by providing shrubbery, gardens or carefully tended balconies, to make up for these inauspicious shapes. Try to soften the rough edges with plants, flowers, trees, anything organic, to occupy the spaces harmoniously.

Now you have your site and blueprint, so the next step is transposing it for the correct compass directions. While the main entrance to your home should be facing south, chances are four-to-one that it will be facing another direction.

So you only have to transpose the 'psychically correct' directions, as explained in the following paragraph, with the actual directions as indicated on your compass.

Once these are ascertained then the attendant four animals will comply with the directions. These are actually symbols (like the mythical animals of the Chinese calendar). The northern (or rear) section of your house is the Tortoise (sacred to China, emblem of longevity, strength and endurance), the buttress, a mountain, hill or building, taller than your own home, for security, safety and stability.

West and East are a Tiger (lord of all animals, emblem of magisterial dignity, model of courage representing autumn and spring). They are embodied by things more down to earth, hills, flowers, trellises, even shady trees.

In front (south) is the Red Phoenix (emperor of all birds, most honourable among the feathered tribes. As it does not prey on living creatures it is acceptable to Buddhists, who disapprove of the taking of life) and should allow for a flat open view, preferably with flowing water. Even if the direction isn't quite south, the ch'i might be coerced by flame-coloured flowers, imaginative landscaping and subtle lighting.

But this is allied to your natural intuition anyhow. When you build within the ch'i pulse you intuitively feel, with the flowing water, flowers, hills and space, that you have what is called the 'armchair configuration'. Secure in the notion that the space behind and to both sides is 'safe'. Your preparation has therefore come to a successful conclusion.

Samuel Beckett wrote, 'I have never been on my way anywhere, but simply am on my way.' A Chinese landscape implies the way rather than the goal.

4

COMPASS

Direction, and Your Inner Aspirations

"Happiness is achieved", said one quirky Chinese poet, "by changing 27 things in your life". Feng shui happiness though starts by changing everything. This happy task is called 'cleaning out your clutter'. This is an essential duty without drudgery. Since your mind and your closets accumulate endless possessions during a lifetime, you're urged to clean out the inessentials. Transpose your mind to that of an older child, choosing favourite toys from a box, jam-packed with playthings.

The dragon's significance is so vital that its portrayal should evoke in the viewer an emotional power. Anything less would be an act of virtual lesé majesté.

The Chinese have a rich history of bridge building. Contrary to overpasses elsewhere, their approach to bridging space is more fanciful than workaday, serving as components within a landscape or as vantages from which to contemplate a pastoral scene.

You should begin this cleansing process with an open, even mirthful mood. Before even dusting a corner, buy (or pluck – should you be so fortunate to own a garden) some fragrant flowers, throw open your windows to fresh air, or maybe spray natural citrus or place a bowl of orange peels on the windowsill.

Music is recommended: A Mozart string quartet, Tubular Bells, Tibetan horns, Ella Fitzgerald. Indulge in a dollop of caviar or prepare an expensive chocolate as a small reward after cleaning each room.

When ready and mentally prepared, don't deliberately make a list. Go to each space spontaneously, holding the object in question to the light, and ask: "Do I still love it? Do I need it? Does it support me? What thoughts do I have when I see it? What thoughts will I have once it's out of my system?"

Ask these questions about fraternity-pins, old photos, bed sheets, shoes and ships and sealing wax. All extraneous objects. If the mood is joyous, the answers will be right. If not so joyous, halt the exercise. No need to force things. The process could take a few hours or a few weeks, but at the end your house will not be empty but filled instead with good things; 'your' things. And you begin with what the ancient Greeks called a tabula blanca – a clean slate.

This is the middle step between Form/Landscape and the arcane Compass School.

The final step is the most complicated and controversial. As mentioned before, the two main schools of feng shui are Form/Landscape and Compass. The former is intuitive and rational. The latter entails the use of two tools – a compass and an octagonal disk – as well as the arcane 'magic' created by the priestly class.

First, make a basic floor plan of the rooms in your house, showing also all points of ventilation, the doors and windows doing a separate plan for each story in the house. The dimensions can be approximate – but the directional relations of each section should be as accurate as possible.

The next step is to find the exact centre of each floor. As noted before, Chinese homes were traditionally rectangular, the centre was then an easy computation.

From the point of view of our complicated architecture today, you'll have to imagine or draw a series of rectangles and ask a geometry teacher to help locate the centres.

You find the directions of your house through the lo-pan Chinese compass. This instrument has five or six circles, with symbols for constellations, negative and positive fortune-points and trigrams from the I-Ching. Those, though, are for the geomancer. The only essential circle that concerns us is in the centre: the compass, with a floating magnetic marker pointing north. Any conventional compass may be used, but the Chinese feng shui compass is a charming objet d'art worth having for the living room table, and an inexpensive bargain from any Chinatown souvenir shop.

The third step is with the pa-kua (or bagua), Chinese for eight numbers. It is an octagonal disk with the eight directions (N, NW, W, SW, S, SE, E, NE), as well as other markers around the yin-yang symbol of Taoism. It is actually an energy 'map', though the directions are only the first marker. You lay the pa-kua down on the centre of your floor plan, with the North sign coinciding with the north direction of your house.

Now you begin to read this map as best you can. Each direction, pointing to the different rooms in the house, will have other markers. They will include the three lines of the I-Ching, a symbol (water, mountain, thunder, wind, fire, earth, lake, heaven), one of the five elements (earth, wood, fire, metal, water), an auspicious number, and possibly the name of a family member, as well as a different colour.

Different geomancers will invariably interpret the readings, like a newspaper editorial, in various ways, but the following simplified codex of these so-called eight Aspirations (with suggestions for the use of the rooms) lists the customary ones.

A stylised fish-dragon roof tile is an auspicious symbol of regeneration, abundance and the wisdom of letters.

(Next page) Examples of the feng shui compass, traditionally inscribed with more than 16 concentric circles.

51

Southeast: Spacious rooms. Wealth, fulfilment. (Enlarged with mirrors).

Aquariums should usher in fortune.

South: Fame. Your study or your office. Fireplace, flowers, water scenes, world maps

Southwest: The bedroom. Happiness: Double images (two vases, two candlesticks, a double bed), quartz to refract soft lights and candles. Peach is the ideal colour. Try to locate to the rear of the house for security.

East: Your library. Wisdom. Scrapbooks. The kids area.

West: Indulge in a great kitchen. Pleasure. Embrace all the fire, water, earth, metal etc., that you will feel comfortable with.

Northeast: The living room or a large dining room. Family. R e l a x i n g, green colour tones. Pictures painted by your kids, photos of relatives and friends. Heirlooms. Fresh plants but no artificial flowers.

North: A room for planning, for contemplating.

Career. Flowing water considered as restorative and emulating our lives in motion.

Northwest: Children's bedroom, their play area. A yang setting for their activities – but keep one corner soft and subdued for the yin time of repose. Clocks, earthy colours, and cream tones.

A ninth direction is most important, (the Emperor's dragon – remember) which is symbolized by the number 5. This is the mystical Centre, which implies Health: Health should pervade all areas of the house. If you have space, a kind of courtyard garden, lacking that, perhaps a verdant rug with an abundance of

flowery and yellow objects. Yellow represents the Earth, from whence our health comes. It is China's national colour and sacred to the emperor.

Health is also vital for cities. The most important Chinese-influenced cities are laid out in a feng shui like grid. The Centre is vitally important. Beijing's centre is the Throne of the Forbidden City (the Emperor being the Dragon). Bangkok's centre is not quite the Grand Palace, but a minuscule temple across the street. Wherever this centre lies, it is vital to the health of the city, which is as organic as the body or the home.

How literal then are these readings? Bear in mind that the Compass School is the mystical discipline of feng shui. Like religious fundamentalists, the Compass School takes the directional elements literally. Others use these directions as teachings, offering a physical and consequently a psychological warmth to your heart, your home or your office.

Feng shui in the office follows the same principles as the home, but here the CEO (or manager) will impose his personal element. One excellent example is

I.M. Pei's architecture at the Louvre. Pei points out, "In Chinese culture water is an auspicious and restorative force". His giant glass pyramid is the Fire shape. But the flames it generates are neutralized by the facing flat 'water' element, of the original Louvre building.

Traditionally, the office, or the series of offices should be square (or at least a portion of a square room) but try avoiding any sharp poison arrows. They should be deflected by a plant, a mirror, maybe a discreet wind chime.

Your Eight aspirations might transform the usual elements as follows:

Southeast: Wealth (CEO or, if he's on another floor, the accounting department)

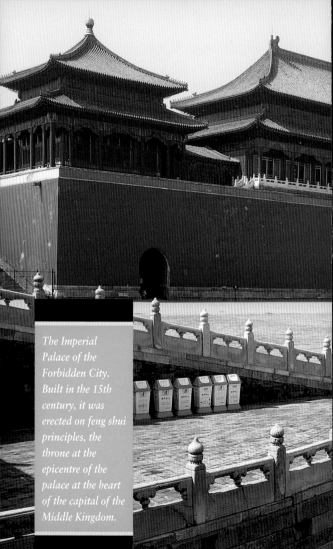

The Imperial Palace of the Forbidden City. Built in the 15th century, it was erected on feng shui principles, the throne at the epicentre of the palace at the heart of the capital of the Middle Kingdom.

Colours of the
Forbidden City were
predominantly red,
the Yang colour
of fire, and yellow,
the national
colour sacred to
the Emperor.

South: Fame (Public relations or press office)
Southwest: Happiness (Chairman of
the Board)
East: Wisdom (Senior executives with
ample experience)
West: Pleasure (Lunchroom, water-cooler,
pastel colours)
Northeast: Family (Human resources
department, affability)
North: Career (Boardroom for unobstructed
planning, clear vision)
Northwest: New directions (Advertising/
image department, IT communications)
Centre: Well-being (Gymnasium, spa,
water, bamboo)

Play around with the angles according to these traits. Place your files in the southeast corner, pictures of your wife and kids in the northwest, pictures of your lover in the southwest. Plants, fish, globes, wherever you obtain the energy from!

A few additional hints: Mirrored windows are to be avoided; they only deflect the ch'i. Desks should face the door, but allow enough space that visitors feel comfortable. Never sit with your back to the door. Stabbing in the back, whether literal or political, occidental or oriental is an age-old business.

Finally, whether for home or office, feng shui is to your benefit. No matter what the charts advise, don't alter anything unless the change is something you love!

'Yu' implies both 'fish' and 'prosperity', propitious feng shui elements. Owing to their reproductive fecundity fish became emblematic of the joys of union – especially of a sexual nature.

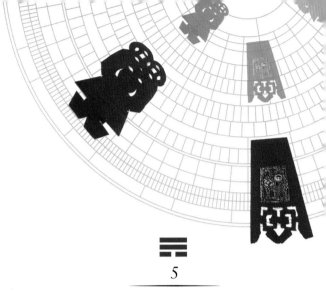

5

SOLUTIONS

Bells, Chimes and Mirrors

Feng shui objects have symbolic and aesthetic values, but the endless assemblage of charms, pictures and talismans, when placed correctly, improve any environment. To quote an old song, they 'accentuate the positive, eliminate the negative'.

First, they can serve as an antidote if your house is not perfectly proportioned. In classical Chinese times, houses were built with regular proportions, so ch'i energy could effortlessly circulate itself. Today, houses are more complex, built to

Rooftop sculpture of the serene Lunar Goddess holding her reflective orb. At day's end, villagers sought refuge behind their fortress-like walls, each connected by inner-courtyards in strict accordance with feng shui principles.

individual tastes, so one must fake or trick the energy to flow in the most propitious channels.

Let's say that one floor of your house is irregular in shape or has too large an area. In this case, you can 'divide' the floor on your miniature grid. Make one area regular, then shape another grid for another room which doesn't quite 'fit in' with what

you require. Your compass and pah-kua readings will basically be the same, so you can create more workable areas.

If you have an 'empty space' that lacks character, employ symbols and play a practical joke on the ch'i, for instance placing a mirror strategically so it reflects a more interesting part of the room, the corridor or reflects the outside garden into the interior.

If an important room is dominated by fire

objects you can neutralize this in the other part of the room with metal. Since fire melts metal, your ch'i will simply overlook that empty space.

The remedies are endless, your imagination boundless, but you don't want to convert your house into a Chinese temple, or an odd curiosity shop. Instead, you want to limit these remedies

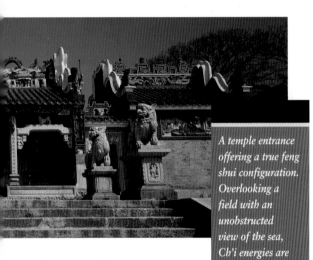

A temple entrance offering a true feng shui configuration. Overlooking a field with an unobstructed view of the sea, Ch'i energies are able to circulate unhindered.

so that your house remains attractive, as well as being 'correct' energy-wise. Rather than rules use imagination and creativity as well as traditional wisdom.

Below are a few of the eight remedies. No matter what your geomancer decrees, feel free to rely on your own instincts and choose your own.

a. Bright objects, like mirrors, lights and crystals. Mirrors should be placed strategically to offer

curving illusions if there are too many formal lines. Or, should two doors be opposite each other, a mirror might offer the illusion of more space. Mirrors need not simply reflect, but through convex and concave surfaces, can provide a pleasing distortion. Crystals (which have made a dynamic New Age comeback) and lights are used for slowing down or accelerating ch'i energies.

But they also send interesting shadows and lights through any room space.

b. Music is a collection of pleasing sounds, 'drawing phoenixes from the sky'. Music can be natural nature sounds or emanating from the radio. Thus, fountains, bubbling aquarium aerators, breezes through an open window, wind chimes and birdsong are all music to the ear and ideal feng shui. The hollow shape of a flute has the double advantage of being musical and a vent for ch'i. Anything pleasing, calming and harmonious to the listener is good feng shui.

c. Moving objects: Mobile paper objects, fountains and fans. When moving gently, they stir the ch'i to circulate about the room. Also in this category are flags, incense, flowing water,

the flicker of a candle, prayer-flags. Plants caught in a cross wind are perfect feng shui.

d. Heavy objects: In the garden, boulders, stones, statues, sculptures slow down the energy level, allowing one time to stroll and absorb the peace and the scents of the garden.

e. Living objects: Plants and animals are preferable to artificial replicas, but both are in feng shui terms accepted. Some 'fake' animals such as fish (the word 'yu' in Chinese means both fish and prosperity) are prized before others. Fish are symbolically employed as the emblem of wealth or abundance. It is also the sign of harmony and connubial bliss. Fish are reputed to swim in pairs, emblematic of the joys of union (especially

of a sexual nature). Fish can be represented either in a painting or alive in an aquarium.

f. Colours: Your own birth date or kua colour could form the theme, but any pleasing combinations are acceptable. Bright reds, whites, greens are all yang

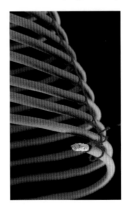

colours, giving energy to shadowy places. Cooler yin tones will soften the mood and provide the ch'i with a melancholic, more moderate pace.

g. Stillness: A statue of the Buddha. A Japanese Zen bowl, a ceramic frog or turtle, a pleasing wall hanging. A calligrapher's brush. A scroll.

h. Aromas: Scented candles, fruit, incense, home cooking, bath salts, freshly washed linen.

i. Curved lines: Ch'i abhors straight lines, so add something organic to that arrow-straight corridor or spacious living room. A bamboo reed or flute, a scroll or ceramic wine-jar, a Japanese tansu, or even a Zu-ming Tai-chi sculpture.

The most important thing is that the objects are not alien but that they reflect you. Almost everything can serve as a feng shui symbol, so long as it brings harmony, peace and beauty to your home. Making you feel at home and not banished or alienated from it because of ill-interpreted laws is precisely what feng shui aims to achieve.

The notorious Fu Dog represents the fierce Yang spirit, there to repel Yin forces, said to be the harbingers of darker omens. Key to the animal's efficacy is its bulging eyes; the more fierc they look, the better they guard.

Han-Shan in the 8th century wrote: "If you ask me how to get to Cold Mountain, I say there is no way to get there. Yes, I went to Cold Mountain, but you'll never reach it by following my path. Your heart and mine are not alike."

A Chinese village: Mountains protect its rear, low hills embrace both flanks. Reasons for such configurations were strategic, offering defences from behind, with a view to survey approaching strangers.

Yin and Yang in Your Own Backyard

Home is where the feng shui heart lies, but it can be interpreted to every life situation from cradle to grave. Modern writers suggest feng shui solution for theatre seats ("Don't sit in a box"), restaurants ("Private booths are best, since you have the turtle to your back") and beauty salons (California hairdressers insist that the length of a woman's hair can be determined by a pa-kua – but that's California!)

Feng shui had its origins in determining propitious locations of graves, which should face both the salubrious southern wind and distant water. But since birth and

(Above)
A rural gravesite.

Chinese garden with moongate. The shape of these notable gates was often decreed by feng shui practitioners, to allow visual access to the hills, the vegetation and flowing waters.

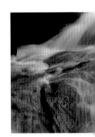

death are part of the same yin-yang process, the geomancer would first have to determine, from the deceased's date of birth and birthplace, the direction and time when the soul is released from the body. Should the feng shui be disregarded or predicted incorrect, then the spirit will float endlessly between heaven

and earth, returning to the family at the most inconvenient times.

Flowers on the graves traditionally should bloom in Chinese gardens, though today this is

largely disregarded. The feng shui garden still exists, with one prime American example in Staten Island, New York. It should be octagonal in shape and should embrace the same layout as the

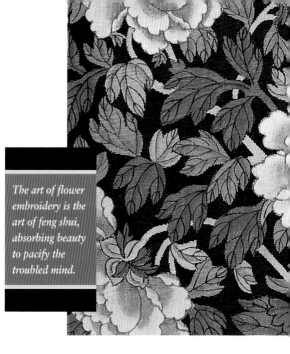

The art of flower embroidery is the art of feng shui, absorbing beauty to pacify the troubled mind.

home: mountains to the north, gentle hills in the east, water and smaller hills in the west, and an empty space and flowing water in the south.

Writer Richard Craze describes the contents: "In the West, we think a garden is completed when we can't plant any more plants into it. In China, a garden is finished when you can't take anything away".

Making a Chinese garden, even in a small section of your backyard, requires a few basic rules. Since a garden is yin, try to engage rounded forms. Circular walkways, rounded arches, curling benches, tree-based non-metallic fences are essential, but they should be shaded with rounded

shrubs. Pathways are important, and natural gravel
is superior to concrete. Rubbish must be covered
up, either with plants like moss or bamboo, or (and
this is more to Chinese than Western tastes) a
mirror to divert one's sight from rubbish.

Flowers are personal choices, though one should
have plenty of climbing plants, since they allow the
energy to fall and re-circulate. On a practical level,
they'll hide unsightly locations, which are
important, since the garden must always be neat
and tended. Some love the yin willow, the Buddhist
symbol for meekness; it is regarded as a sign of
spring and owing to its beauty, suppleness and
frailty, it has become the emblem of the fair sex.

The lotus, real or
stylised, is the floral
spirit of Asia.
It represents purity,
rising as it does
from the sodden
earth, beautiful
and undefiled.

The female waist is compared to the willow, though some have funereal associations with the willow. The magnolia is the flower that ushers in spring on account of its large white blossoms, which appear before its leaves appear. It is an emblem of feminine sweetness and beauty. Miniature pine trees, always seen in wistful silhouettes on Chinese mountains are symbols of longevity. For garden ponds, nothing is more sacred to Buddhism, the Chinese and to feng shui than the lotus. At the head of all cultivated flowers is the sacred Lotus bud. It's emblematic of summer and fruitfulness, of the Lord Buddha himself who felt that

the lotus, by extending itself in the water, was like the wisdom of the mind. The Buddha is often represented seated on a giant lotus.

Flower position and colour is important. Colour in Chinese symbolism may be emblematic of rank, authority, virtue and vice, joy and sorrow. Red, the emblem of joy, and orange plants, represent the yang so should alternate with green plants. Trees should be delicate and never overshadow the rest of the garden. If you have enough space, the planted flowers should alternate with smaller pot plants. An herb garden is obviously pleasing, for its natural aromatherapy as well as joy in cooking.

While Western gardens accentuate the flowers, a feng shui garden needs non-organic objects to help the energy circulate around the flowers. A few rocks in the middle of paths will slow down the energy. Little hills will take the place of mountains, but some tallish trees will be a fine replacement.

Natural sounds are important. Birds and insects, which figure largely in Chinese symbolism and are to be seen in pictures, chinaware, in bronze or stone and as architectural relief. The wind around a series of bells, the mini-rippled charm of a tiny rock goldfish pond.

Try to include the Five Elements. The pond is

Water, a sundial is Metal, shrubs are Wood, red flowers are Fire and for Earth, well, the earth.

If the garden is right, a sunset stroll will lead to friendship, love, marriage and family. But beware how you relate to that significant 'other'. If you are Water, then the red azaleas may inflame you, but if your partner is Fire, then such a hot colour could lead to unromantic excesses.

A few hints from popular music:

'Three Coins in a Fountain' is pure feng shui. Water is romance, Metal is one of the five elements bringing harmony. 'Red Sails in the Sunset' have an equal effect. Red being the colour of joy, passion and romance (Chinese brothels have red lights in the window, as in the movie 'Raise the Red Lantern'), sails are guided by winds, and gentle winds in a restricted space keep the ch'i moving. (Hong Kong has a feng shui name, since the words mean 'fragrant harbour', and that should

Earth

Fire

bring prosperity). If the winds are stagnant, the love energy needs cosmic Viagra. If the winds and air are open and un-hindered, then so is love. Barbara Streisand's 'People Who Need People' should be changed to Fire People Who Need Water People etc.

Metal

The bedroom must be individually convivial for each of the five different elements of lovers. Fire people are passionate, Earth people stable, Water people creative and emotional, Metal people rigid and

Wood

serious and Wood folks are expansive.

But when all is well, when the garden and bedroom lead to love and marriage, then it's time to build a little feng shui cottage.

Water

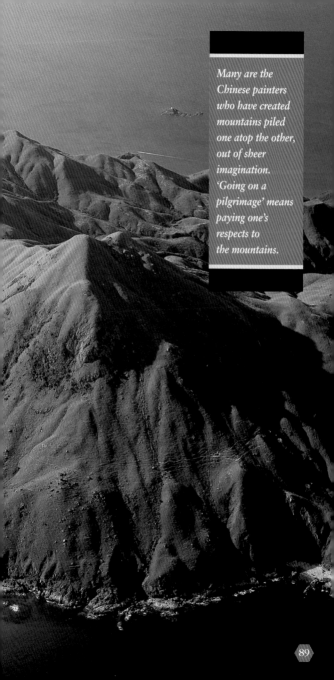

Many are the
Chinese painters
who have created
mountains piled
one atop the other,
out of sheer
imagination.
'Going on a
pilgrimage' means
paying one's
respects to
the mountains.

7

ART

The Energy and the Ecstasy

Feng shui is an art in itself, but its influence on the arts, both Occidental and Oriental, is considerable, if sometimes unwitting and unaware.

Architecture is of course the essence of feng shui. But painting has been as much a part of feng shui as cenotaphs and house shapes.

Early paintings during the Han Period (206 BCE-220 CE) included magical Taoist symbols, just as

Christian symbols were always part of pre-Renaissance Western art. What is apparently a landscape painting will contain objects that are seemingly incongruous, including dragons and turtles. All these symbols display humankind existing amidst a rationally configured nature. The paintings are less aesthetic creations and more teachings.

In Chinese calligraphy, students are taught to trust the intuitive flow of the hand, aligning ch'i universal energy with their inspiration. Feng shui has given

Calligraphy, where each stroke embodies the ch'i of the artist.

Door Gods, with their fierce visages and battle dress, originally stood guard outside palace doors. At Chinese New Year, faded images are today given a 'retirement' and replaced with fresh renderings.

the name to that popular Chinese martial art, Tai ch'i, or 'great energy'.

Ancient Chinese classical music shares feng shui's fascination with symbols. No less than 84 different scale combinations were laid out, each as the basis for a different religious ceremony with different classes of nobles. Neither inspiration nor emotion was part of the music. Instead, it was 'correct' music to allow 'unseen energies' to animate the listener.

On the same note, so to speak, the Chinese orchestra is based on the feng shui Eight Categories, dependent on the material of the instruments. These are bells (Metal), chimes (stone), ocarinas (Earth), drums (skin), zithers (silk), percussion blocks (Wood), mouth organs (gourd) and flutes (bamboo).

While geomancers insist on putting food in the medical category, a good Chinese meal is an art in itself. The art, though, is based on yin and yang, the sugar and spice of cuisine. Both body and nutrient have their positive and negative qualities. Sixth century writer Sun Tze-miao wrote that doctors prescribe food first, if that fails, then a dose of medicine. But banquets take yin and yang seriously. Every dish has its 'cool' and 'hot' essences and should be balanced accordingly.

Yin, the feminine aspect, appears in the most delicate vegetables. Turnips, squash, soybeans, potatoes, all choi leaves are yin. When food is boiled, making it softer, more pliable, the recipes are yin. Milk and other dairy products are rare in southern Chinese food, but this too has a yin aspect, as does ginseng. The only yin meat is pork, coming from that most somnolent of barnyard animals.

Yang dishes are more 'outgoing', aggressive, perhaps not as healthy. Wine is certainly yang, as is beef and chicken. Garlic, ginger, green/red peppers, other 'exciting' vegetables are all yang.

Should you feel anaemic, yang dishes will help

to balance the yin temperament. More virulent diseases like a sore throat or measles? Yin dishes will ease the body.

But few today are aware of the ancient 'philosophical last course', a rare practice placing it firmly in the category of feng shui art.

Traditionally, it is bad luck to partake of the

last morsel from any of the succeeding platters at a banquet. Thus, the remnants of each plate are returned to the kitchen and passed on to the maître – the Father of the Kitchen. He will blend these vestiges of the banquet and use his imagination and artifice to prepare a unique recipe.

It was said that the philosopher Mencius claimed this dish was most pleasing to Heaven, since it combined yin and yang, it had never appeared before in all eternity, and could never again be duplicated. It was, in other words, a yin/yang blending of Chance and Fate. All of which sounds very profound, until you recognize that Mencius is describing common old chop suey!

Coiled incense is visually appealing and personal, as it identifies, by a red tag, the name of the donor. Joss sticks on the other hand (from the Portuguese 'deus' or god) are simply swept from the altar each night.

As the dragon is the Emperor, so the phoenix is the Empress. As a bird embraced by the Buddhist faith, it feeds on grain and appears only in times of peace.

☷

8

SCIENCE

The Universe
Next Door

Feng shui can be classified as religion, art, ritual or interior decoration... it can also be easily compared to contemporary quantum physics.

Both physicists and feng shui geomancers developed tools to divine the future, but these tools are by definition inadequate, since there are no real rules. The physicist has blackboards crammed with numbers and equations – all attempting to explain the unexplainable through a virtual model. The feng shui geomancer has the tools of kua, birth dates, directions and elements. But even to the devoted geomancer, these are only probabilities, convenient Chinese boxes in which to place the infinite enigmas of the enigmatic universe.

Nor is it an exaggeration to show that the innate characteristics of feng shui are present in other kinds of science today. Physicists assert that matter can be both particles and waves simultaneously. Ch'i energy is a continuous wave, but the particles may change as they encounter different spaces and objects.

The yin-yang dichotomy can be akin to the left and right spheres of the brain. The right is yin, seeing whole patterns, intuitive, feeling. The left is logic, causal, with exact routes, the yang masculine.

Modern physics also sees, without problems, a 'parallel universe', since nothing is really objective in this universe. Feng shui creates entire parallel universes in the corner of a room. A fish may be either a picture or an organism, but since both are illusions, they serve the same purpose. And both can inhabit a palpable, material – but just-out-of-reach – universe next door.

Post-Einstein quantum physics infers that by simply observing something, we change it and it in turn changes us. Feng shui offers the same concept. Those who don't practice feng shui may enter a room and admire its ambiance. Those who have an inkling of what feng shui is will enter the same room and have a greater sensitivity to that energy which gives the room that feeling. It will be a change, a harmony, a sense of well-being.

Psychoanalysis, like feng shui, does not provide a solution, but prompts, suggests, waits for the solution to arrive from the patient/practitioner. Again like feng shui, psychoanalysis says that answers to problems are within, not without – and that 'cleaning out the clutter' will expose ideas which may have been hibernating in the deeper recesses of the mind. The purpose of the therapist is not to 'correct' the patient, but to prompt and suggest, to wait for the patient himself to find the solution.

In the endless regions of what Buddhists call 'the great ocean of the mind', one recalls the lines of e.e. cummings:

for whatever we lose (like a you or a me)
it's always ourselves we find in the sea.

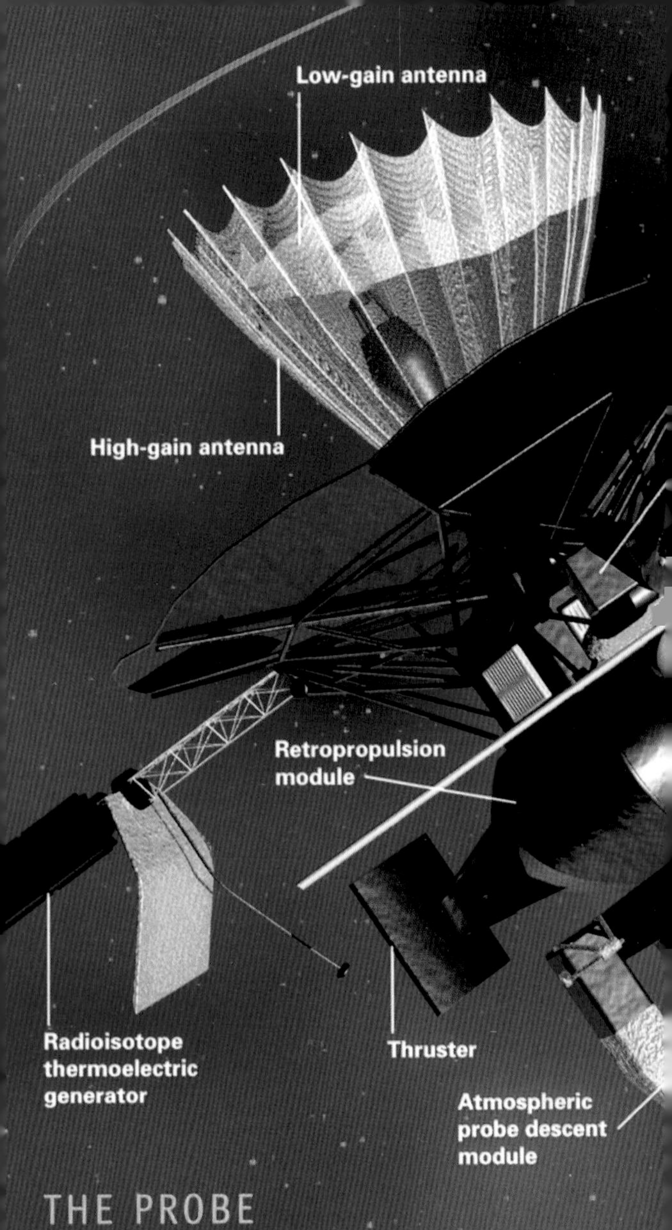

Low-gain antenna

High-gain antenna

Retropropulsion module

Radioisotope thermoelectric generator

Thruster

Atmospheric probe descent module

THE PROBE

Five months before Galileo reached Jupiter, the craft's atmo-spheric probe was released on a trajectory that would eventually

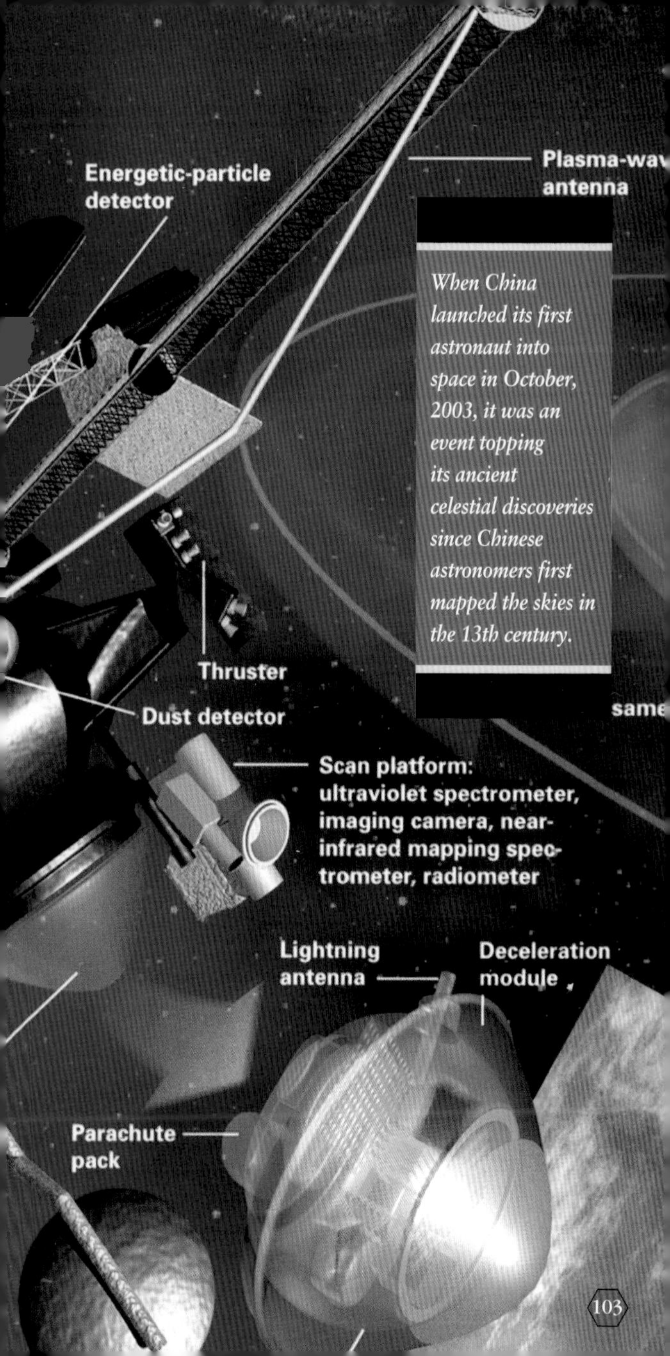

Energetic-particle
detector

Plasma-wave
antenna

When China
launched its first
astronaut into
space in October,
2003, it was an
event topping
its ancient
celestial discoveries
since Chinese
astronomers first
mapped the skies in
the 13th century.

Thruster

Dust detector

same

Scan platform:
ultraviolet spectrometer,
imaging camera, near-
infrared mapping spec-
trometer, radiometer

Lightning
antenna

Deceleration
module

Parachute
pack

9

POSTLUDE

Words of Caution and Joy

By definition, no proof of invisible ch'i exists, although scientists measuring brain-wave 'joy factors' may someday determine whether feng shui configurations do indeed harness special energies.

Unlike philosophies and sciences with sacred books, feng shui has no single text, no Ten Commandments, and, in a way, is as variable as the wind and water which give it its name. Like energy, the 'way' cannot be shown, true. But clouds find their own 'way' with the help of the invisible wind. Water finds its own natural course at its own natural pace. Until the questionable era of giant dams, trying to 'push' water like trying to 'push' paper through a fax machine.

Still, nobody can deny that, with all its rituals and mysteries, feng shui is part of that same perennial philosophy which has inspired Sufi poetry, Kabalistic numerology and the poetry of Blake. All of them assert that energy comes through the cosmic winds of the ether, embracing our atmosphere and our lives.

Artists and poets instinctively have this energy. For the rest of us, feng shui is, in its simplest terms, a practical way to use it.

Can we, after thousands of books, translations and interpretations, really understand this field of energy and dreams? The philosopher Friedrich Hegel said of himself, "Only one person in the world understands me. And even he doesn't understand me". Understanding, though, is secondary to the joy of feng shui. And that joy is the opposite of rigidity.

A fundamentalist feng shui believer once berated a friend who had left his golf clubs in his perfectly configured room, almost shouting, "Take them away. They're straight. They're letting in the Poison Arrows". Obviously he didn't understand that feng shui must preserve harmonies among people as well as furniture. Nor did he comprehend that after 8,000 years of priests, charlatans and sages, the configurations, calendars and compasses are only machinery, of little importance in themselves.

Still, sceptics query whether feng shui is science or art. Like yang and yin, it is both. The rules are suggestions, not certainties. The predictions are guides, not truths. And the essence might come from the images created by the 11th century poet Fan Chung-yen. In two metaphorical lines, he gives us an architectural painting embracing the gentle energy of our universe, our homes and ourselves:

"Poolside pavilions are the first
to see our moon:
Flowers near the sun are announcing
our spring."

Since ancient times it has been customary to cleanse one's mind and body prior to approaching a location of spirituality. The characters on the square well interpret as, 'It is sufficient in life to know oneself'.